Edgings
for Kids

Edgit™ US Patent

M000248020

LEISURE ARTS, INC. • Maumelle, Arkansas

Meet the Designer:
Cony Larsen

Cony Larsen of Highland, Utah, is a designer and author of crochet books and tools. Describing her style as Boho Chic with a touch of traditional, Cony says she loves projects that can be finished in a day or two, and finds inspiration in the children in her life, her garden, and her love of hand-loomed textiles and fibers. For more about her designs, tools, and aid programs for her Guatemalan homeland, visit her website, conylarsenbooks.com.

Introduction

Crochet edgings can transform plain and simple blankets, bibs, and clothing into colorful gifts that will delight children and parents alike. The **Edgit™ Piercing & Crochet Hooks** included in this book allow you to crochet on the edge in one step, without having to pre-punch holes in the fabric. Then the standard hook that is included can be used to finish the work. Even if you've never crocheted before, you can learn with our easy "Don't make me think!" illustrated step-by-step instructions. A wide variety of projects are shown to inspire you in making gifts of love for the little ones in your life.

EDITORIAL STAFF
Senior Product Director: Pam Stebbins
Creative Art Director: Katherine Laughlin
Technical Writer: Sarah J. Green
Technical Editors: Linda A. Daley, Cathy Hardy, and Lois J. Long
Editorial Writer: Susan Frantz Wiles
Art Category Manager: Lora Puls
Graphic Artist: Jessica Bramlett
Prepress Technician: Stephanie Johnson

BUSINESS STAFF
President and Chief Executive Officer: Fred F. Pruss
Senior Vice President of Operations: Jim Dittrich
Vice President of Retail Sales: Martha Adams
Chief Financial Officer: Tiffany P. Childers
Controller: Teresa Eby
Information Technology Director: Brian Roden
Director of E-Commerce: Mark Hawkins
Manager of E-Commerce: Robert Young

Edgit™ US Patent Pending Piercing Hook

ISBN-13/EAN: 978-1-4647-1683-6

Contents

2 | Meet the Designer: Cony Larsen

4 | General Instructions

   4 Basic Tools and Supplies

   4 Crocheting Around Corners

   5 Finishing Your Project

   6 Preparing Your Fabric

   7 How to Crochet on the Edge

   8 Foundation Rounds

9 | Fancy Edgings

   10 Fancy Princess

   12 Over the Rainbow

   13 Sweet Pea

   14 Bonjour Butterfly

   16 Duck, Duck

   17 So Berry Scallops

18 | Lullaby Edgings

   19 Under the Sea Shells

   20 Lucy Locket

   21 XoXo

   22 Rockabye

   23 Tiny Back Steps

   24 Twists 'n Twirls

25 | Baby Shower Edgings

   26 Li'l Sunshine

   27 Sophia

   28 Ethan

   29 Noah

   30 Olivia

   31 Aiden

32 | On the Edge Crochet

   33 Very Berry

   34 Dainty Blossoms

   35 Sweet Lullaby

   36 All Bliss

   37 Soft Cuddles

   38 Just Dreamy

40 | Just Dreamy Edgings

   41 African Flower

   42 Crescent Seashells Apron

   43 Reversible Bandana Pocket Full of Posies

   44 Butterfly Wings Pillowcase

   45 Rosebloom Cross Fans

   46 Apple Green Trellis Summer Dress

   47 Reversible Tulips Peter Pan Collar

48 | Stitch Guide

General Instructions

Read all instructions before you start working on your project. Make sure you have the basic tools and supplies handy. Read the pattern instructions and make sure you understand them.

Basic Tools and Supplies

✧ Edgit™ Piercing & Crochet Hooks. If you're using pre-hemstitched or pre-punched fabric, you only need hook size 4/1.75mm.

✧ Fingering or 4 ply yarn: 7-8 sts per inch (2.5 cm), or 1 Ball/50g of DMC® Cebelia Crochet Cotton thread #5 or #10; see individual patterns for yarn or thread required.

✧ Fabric: To make a double-sided blanket 40" x 40" (101.5 cm x 101.5 cm) with flannel or cotton, you will need $1\frac{1}{8}$ yards (1.125 meters) for each side of blanket; ¾ yard (.75 meter) for each side will yield 2-3 bibs or burps.

Foundation Rounds

Unless otherwise instructed, make sure to crochet both foundation rounds before crocheting your pattern; see pages 7 and 8.

Crocheting Around Corners

Please note that if your crochet tension is tight, you will need to crochet additional scs around the corners on Foundation Round 1; this will prevent your corners from curling up. To do this, crochet two sc in every other hole around the corner on Foundation Round 1 only, rather than just one sc in each hole. If your crochet tension is loose or relaxed, you should be fine crocheting one sc in each hole on Foundation Round 1.

FAQ - Will the Edgit™ Piercing Hook work with pre-hemstitched fabric?

The Edgit™ Piercing Hook will work with pre-hemstitched or pre-punched fabric; however, you might want to use the Edgit™ Crochet Hook instead; since the holes are already made on pre-hemstitched fabric, you really don't need a piercing hook for it.

We have made many efforts to ensure that our instructions are accurate. However, we cannot be responsible for human errors, typographical mistakes, or variations in individual work. Basic sewing and crochet knowledge are required.

Finishing Your Project

Steam Blocking

What a great sense of accomplishment there is when a crochet project is finally completed! Though a relatively simple technique, blocking is what gives many projects a polished appearance. The process shapes and sets the design and smooths the stitches into place. Steam blocking is great for lots of crochet projects. Here are some handy tips we've learned over the years about blocking:

First, you should always check the yarn label for any special care instructions. Many natural fibers, such as cotton, linen, and wool, respond well to steam blocking. However, you shouldn't use steam or heat on mohair or angora.

There are also many acrylics and some blends that shouldn't be blocked at all, especially with steam because they might melt.

Second, you will need a fluffy hand towel or handkerchief and a padded ironing board. If you prefer, you can substitute a table or any flat surface that you have padded adequately.

Take the dampened fluffy towel or handkerchief, place it over the edge of the project, and steam with an iron, holding the iron slightly above your project. Lift the towel and repeat with another section all the way around. Finally, leave the item in place until it's dry.

Preparing Your Fabric

Measure and Cut

Follow instructions on your sewing pattern. If you are using one of Ammee's free download patterns for the **Apron**, **Summer Dress**, **Bandana, Skirt,** or **Peter Pan Collar**, follow these instructions to prepare the side where you will be working your crochet edge. If you are using your own sewing pattern, or an item that is already made, such as pillowcases, you will need to follow these instructions too.

To make a double-sided blanket 40" x 40" (101.5 cm x 101.5 cm) with flannel or cotton, you will need 1⅛ yards (1.125 meters) for each side of blanket. With wrong sides together, measure and cut blanket to desired size.

Cut Rounded Corners

(optional step): After cutting your blanket to the desired size, fold blanket in half and then in half again; use a plate as a pattern and place it on the corner of folded fabric where the corners meet, and cut excess fabric off to round the corners.

Step 1: (Optional) This step will prevent fabric from raveling while you crochet. With wrong sides together, serge around the entire edge of your project. If you don't own a serger, use any stitch option on your sewing machine.

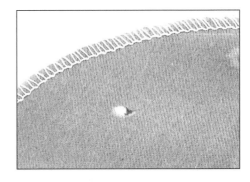

Spacing Between Holes: The distance between each zigzag should be about ⅛" (3 mm). Test different settings on your machine until you achieve the desired spacing. We set our Length knob on our machine to the 2 setting, and the Width knob to almost 4. Sew this round about ¼" (7 mm) from edge.

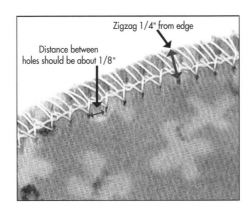

Distance between holes should be about 1/8"

Zigzag 1/4" from edge

Step 2: (Optional) This step will help to space your crochet stitches evenly, and it will be easier to insert your Edgit™ in the holes too. Zigzag around the edge of your blanket; *(see Spacing Between Holes)*. A Hemstitch needle may help to make the holes slightly bigger, see Hemstitch Needle.

Hemstitch Needle (Optional): If your sewing machine does not have a hemstitch stitch option, you may want to replace your regular sewing needle with a Hemstitch Needle #19 by Schmetz to sew bigger holes. **Warning:** Your sewing machine must have a front loading bobbin compartment to use a hemstitch needle.

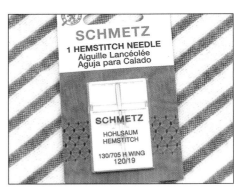

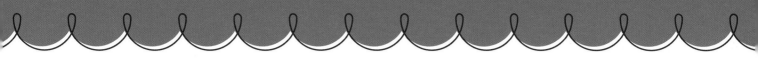

How to Crochet on the Edge

Foundation Rnd 1 -

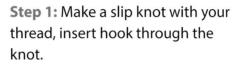

Option 1

Rnd 1: With the Piercing Edgit™, single crochet (sc) in each zigzag hole around entire edge. See Steps 1-4.

Step 1: Make a slip knot with your thread, insert hook through the knot.

Step 2: Insert hook through one of the zigzag holes and draw thread with hook.

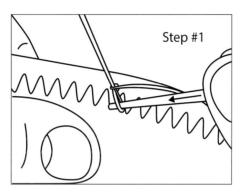

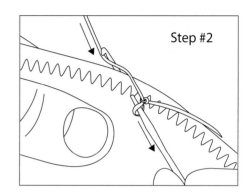

Step 3: Pull thread through the zigzag hole.

Step 4: Draw thread with hook and pull through both loops on the hook.

Completed single crochet (sc). Repeat Steps 2-4, crochet 1 sc in each bottom zigzag hole around. Join with slip stitch to 1st sc.

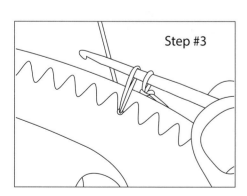

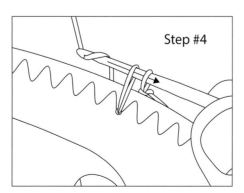

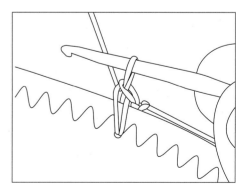

Foundation Rnd 1 -

Option 2
Rnd 1: With the Piercing Edgit™, 2 sc in 1st zigzag hole, *sk next hole, 2 sc in next hole; repeat from * around. Join with sl st to beg sc.

Foundation Rnd 1 -

Option 3
Rnd 1: With the Piercing Edgit™, 2 sc in 1st zigzag hole, *sk next hole, 1 sc in next hole, sk next hole, 2 sc in next hole; repeat from * around. Join with sl st to beg sc.

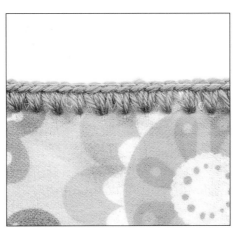

Foundation Rnd 2 -

Rnd 2: Switch to the Edgit™ Crochet Hook, chain 1, sc through both loops of 1st sc, and in each sc around. Join with a slip stitch to beg sc.

Cony's Tips
Crocheting around corners: Please note that if your crochet tension is tight, you will need to crochet additional scs around the corners on Foundation Rnd 1; this will prevent your corners from curling up. To do this, crochet two sc in every other hole around the corner on Foundation Rnd 1 only, rather than just one sc in each hole. If your crochet tension is loose or relaxed, you should be fine crocheting one sc in each hole on Foundation Rnd 1.

Fancy Edgings

These beautiful patterns will tickle you pink! We have illustrated every step to make it easier for beginners and "visual" crafters. Enjoy!

Fancy Princess

INSTRUCTIONS

Note: Use the Edgit™ Piercing Crochet Hook to work Foundation Rnd 1; switch to the Edgit™ Crochet Hook for Rnds 2-6.

Foundation Rnds 1 and 2: Crochet Foundation Rnd 1 - Option 1 and Rnd 2 following instructions on pages 7 and 8.

Rnd 3: Ch 3, (counts as first dc), dc in next 2 sc, *ch 1, sk next sc, dc in next 3 sc*, repeat from * to * around. Join with sl st to beg ch 3.

Rnd 4: Ch 1, sc in same st, *ch 4, sc in ch-1 space*, repeat from * to * around. Join with sl st to beg sc.

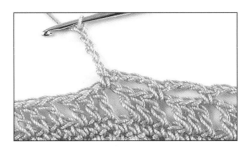

Rnd 5: Ch 1, sc in first ch-4 space, *10 dc in the next ch-4 space, sc in the next ch-4 space; repeat from * around. Join with sl st to beg sc. You can fasten off at the end of this round or you can proceed to do Rnd 6.

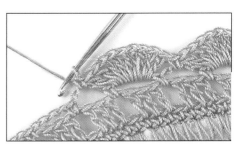

Cony's Tips
Keep it simple.
Plan and read instructions before you get started.
Practice to master the perfect tension.
Find a crochet mentor.
Take a class to learn the basics.
Keep your fibers protected in a yarn/thread dispenser while you work on your project.
Use the right size hooks.

Rnd 6: Ch 1, *sl st in the next 5 dc, ch 3, sl st in the next 5 dc and in sc between scallops*, repeat from * to * around. Join with sl st to beg st. Fasten off. Weave in ends. Block.

RIBBON INSTRUCTIONS

For Blanket: Cut four strands of ribbon, each 45" (114.5 cm) long. Hook a safety pin to one end of a ribbon strand and thread through the ch-3 spaces of Rnd 3; repeat with the other three sides. Tie a bow at each of the four corners where the ends of the ribbon meet.

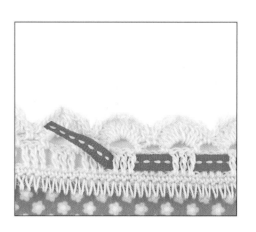

Over the Rainbow

Thread (Size 10)
[1.75 ounces, 284 yards
(50 grams, 260 meters) per ball]:
☐ 1 Ball

Crochet Hooks
☐ Edgit™ Piercing Hook **and**
☐ Edgit™ Crochet Hook

Additional Supplies
☐ See page 4, Basic Tools &
Supplies

INSTRUCTIONS

Note: Use the Edgit™ Piercing
Crochet Hook to work Foundation
Rnd 1; switch to the Edgit™
Crochet Hook for Rnds 2-5.

Foundation Rnds 1 and 2:
Crochet Foundation Rnd 1 -
Option 1 and Rnd 2 following
instructions on pages 7 and 8.

Rnd 3: Ch 1, sc in same st, *ch 3, sk
3 sc, sc in next sc, ch 4, sk 3 sc, sc in
next sc*, repeat from * to * around.
Join with sl st to beg sc.

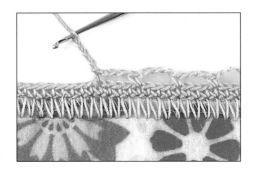

Rnd 4: Ch 1, sc in same st, *sc in
ch-3 space, (5 dc, ch 2, 5 dc) in next
ch-4 space*, repeat from * to *
around. Join with sl st to beg sc.

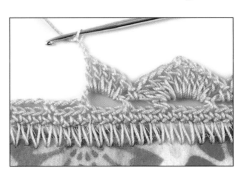

Rnd 5: Ch 1, sc in same st, sk next
sc, *sc in next 5 dc, (sc, ch 2, sc) in
next ch-2 space, sc in next 5 dc, sk
sc between rainbows*, repeat from
* to * around. Join with sl st to beg
sc. Fasten off. Weave in ends. Block.

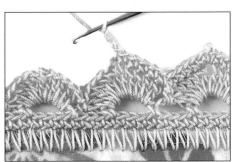

Cony's Tip
Use this elegant crochet
edging for any project.
Work the two foundation
rounds in a different color
for a different look.

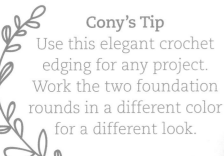

Sweet Pea

Our Sweet Pea pattern is a great pattern
for beginners. It's sweet, fast, and practical.

SHOPPING LIST

Thread (Size 10) **LACE 0**
**[1.75 ounces, 284 yards
(50 grams, 260 meters) per ball]:**
☐ 1 Ball

Crochet Hooks
☐ Edgit™ Piercing Hook **and**
☐ Edgit™ Crochet Hook

Additional Supplies
☐ See page 4, Basic Tools &
Supplies

STITCH GUIDE
PICOT
(Sc, ch 3, sc) in st
indicated.

Rnd 3: Ch 1, *sc in next 2 sc,
crochet a Picot in the next sc*;
repeat from * to * around. Join
with sl st to beg st. Fasten off.
Weave in ends. Block.

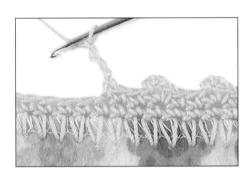

Cony's Tip
I'm always looking for ways to spice up my
crochet projects. I love the variety of embellishments
available — buttons, ribbons, silk flowers. Your local
craft or scrapbook store is a great place for ideas.
Next time you crochet a baby's bib or hat, try adding
some decorations. The choices are endless!

INSTRUCTIONS
Note: Use the Edgit™ Piercing
Crochet Hook to work Foundation
Rnd 1; switch to the Edgit™
Crochet Hook for Rnds 2-3.

Foundation Rnds 1 and 2:
Crochet Foundation Rnd 1 -
Option 1 and Rnd 2 following
instructions on pages 7 and 8.

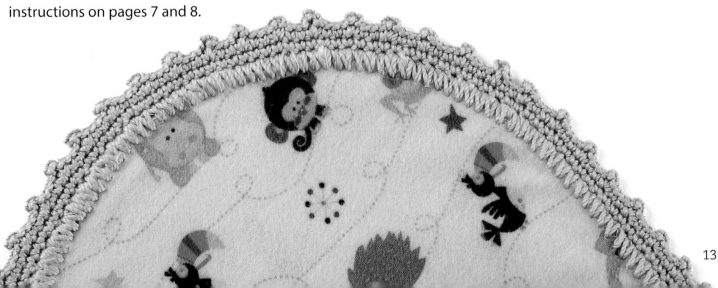

Bonjour Butterfly

Thread (Size 10) **0** LACE
[1.75 ounces, 284 yards
(50 grams, 260 meters) per ball]:
- ☐ 1 Ball

Crochet Hooks
- ☐ Edgit™ Piercing Hook **and**
- ☐ Edgit™ Crochet Hook

Additional Supplies
- ☐ ¼" (7 mm) Wide ribbon -
  5 yards (4.5 meters)
- ☐ Small safety pin
- ☐ See page 4, Basic Tools &
  Supplies

INSTRUCTIONS

Note: Use the Edgit™ Piercing
Crochet Hook to work Foundation
Rnd 1; switch to the Edgit™
Crochet Hook for Rnds 2-6.

Foundation Rnds 1 and 2:
Crochet Foundation Rnd 1 -
Option 1 and Rnd 2 following
instructions on pages 7 and 8.

Rnd 3: Ch 1, sc in same st, sc in
the next 2 sc; *ch 4, sk next 3 sc;
sc in next 3 sc*; repeat from * to *
around. Join with sl st to beg sc.

Rnd 4: Ch 2, sk 1st sc, *sl st in next
sc, sk next sc, [1 sc, 1 hdc, 5 dc,
1 hdc, 1 sc] in next ch-4 space, sk
next sc; repeat from * around. Join
sl st to beg ch.

Rnd 5: *Ch 6, sl st in sl st between
next two petals; rep from * around.
You'll be working the ch-6 behind
the petals; we've folded the front
petal down to show this step. Join
with sl st to beg ch.

Rnd 6: Ch 1, work a petal as follows: *[1 sc, 1 hdc, 2 dc, 3 tr, 2 dc,1 hdc, 1 sc] in next ch-6 space, sk sl st between petals, repeat from * around. Join with sl st to beg ch. Fasten off. Weave in ends. Block.

RIBBON INSTRUCTIONS

For Blanket: Cut four strands of ribbon, each 45" (114.5 cm) long. Hook a safety pin to one end of a ribbon strand and thread through the ch-3 spaces of Rnd 3; repeat with the other three sides. Tie a bow at each of the four corners where the ends of the ribbon meet.

Duck, Duck

INSTRUCTIONS

Note: Use the Edgit™ Piercing
Crochet Hook to work Foundation
Rnd 1; switch to the Edgit™
Crochet Hook for Rnds 2-3.

Foundation Rnds 1 and 2:
Crochet Foundation Rnd 1 -
Option 1 and Rnd 2 following
instructions on pages 7 and 8.

Rnd 3: Ch 2, *sk 3 sc, 6 dc in the
base of next sc, ch 1, sk 3 sc, sl st
in next sc, repeat from * around.
Join with sl st to beg ch. Fasten off.
Weave in ends. Block.

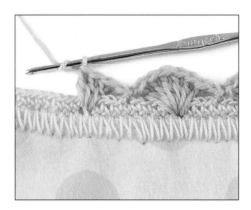

Cony's
VERY IMPORTANT TIP!
Remember, use your
Edgit™ Piercing
Crochet Hook on
the first round of
each project, and then
switch to your
Edgit™ Crochet Hook
for the following
rounds and with
pre-hemstitched
fabrics.

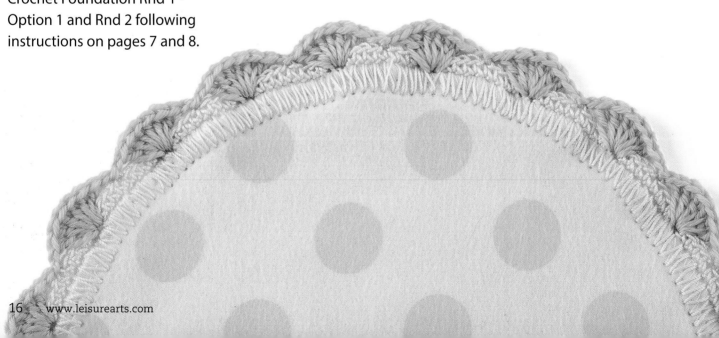

So Berry Scallops

SHOPPING LIST

Thread (Size 10) 🧶 **0** LACE
[1.75 ounces, 284 yards (50 grams, 260 meters) per ball]:
☐ 1 Ball

Crochet Hooks
☐ Edgit™ Piercing Hook **and**
☐ Edgit™ Crochet Hook

Additional Supplies
☐ See page 4, Basic Tools & Supplies

Rnd 3: Ch 1, sc in same st, sc in the next 2 sc; *ch 4, sk next sc, sc in next 3 sc*; rep from * to * around. Join with sl st to beg sc.

Rnd 4: Ch 1, sk first sc, *sc in next sc, sk next sc; 8 sc in ch-4 space; sk next sc; rep from * to * around. Join with sl st to beg st. Fasten off. Weave in ends. Block.

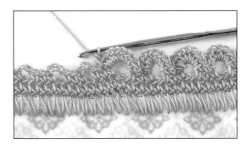

INSTRUCTIONS

Note: Use the Edgit™ Piercing Crochet Hook to work Foundation Rnd 1; switch to the Edgit™ Crochet Hook for Rnds 2-4.

Foundation Rnds 1 and 2: Crochet Foundation Rnd 1 - Option 1 and Rnd 2 following instructions on pages 7 and 8.

Lullaby Edgings

The beauty of a handmade gift is unparalleled. From the time you choose a fabric and plan the edging colors, you must conclude that you are creating a labor of love.

Under the Sea Shells

This pattern requires that you work Rounds 3 and 4 in the base of single crochets rather than through the loops of single crochets.

SHOPPING LIST

Thread (Size 10) **0** LACE
[1.75 ounces, 284 yards
(50 grams, 260 meters) per ball]:
☐ Color #1 (Yellow) - 1 Ball
☐ Color #2 (Pink) - 1 Ball

Crochet Hooks
☐ Edgit™ Piercing Hook **and**
☐ Edgit™ Crochet Hook

Additional Supplies
☐ See page 4, Basic Tools & Supplies

Rnd 3: Join color B in any sc of Rnd 2. Ch 1, working only in the **base** of all single crochets, *sc in next 3 sc, 4 dc in the **base** of next sc from Rnd 1*, repeat from * to * around. Join with sl st to beg sc. Make sure your tension is not too tight or the edge will start to curl.

Rnd 4: Ch 1, sc in same sc and in each sc around. Join with sl st to beg sc. Fasten off. Weave in ends. Block.

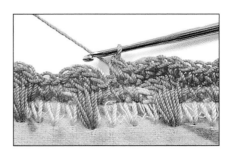

INSTRUCTIONS

Note: Use the Edgit™ Piercing Crochet Hook to work Foundation Rnd 1; switch to the Edgit™ Crochet Hook for Rnds 2-4.

Foundation Rnds 1 and 2: With color #1, crochet Foundation Rnd 1 - Option 1 and Rnd 2 following instructions on pages 7 and 8.

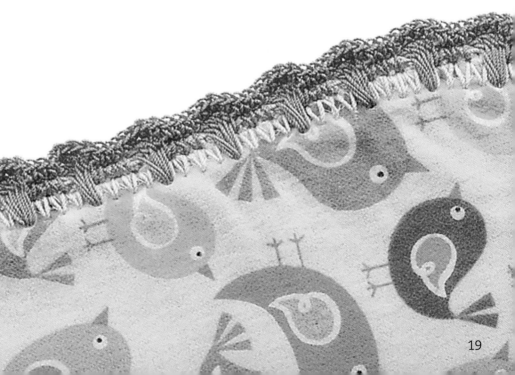

Lucy Locket

Lucy Locket is a nursery rhyme about an ornate, precious metal case that has space for a memento. Our fancy edging will remind you to share this rhyme with a precious little one.

SHOPPING LIST

Yarn (Super Fine Weight) 🧶**1**
[3.5 ounces, 437 yards (100 grams, 400 meters) per skein]:
☐ 1 Skein
You may also use any yarn that will yield 7-8 sts per inch (2.5 cm).

Crochet Hooks
☐ Edgit™ Piercing Hook **and**
☐ Edgit™ Crochet Hook

Additional Supplies
☐ See page 4, Basic Tools & Supplies

INSTRUCTIONS

Note: Use the Edgit™ Piercing Crochet Hook to work Foundation Rnd 1; switch to the Edgit™ Crochet Hook for Rnds 2-5.

Foundation Rnds 1 and 2:
Crochet Foundation Rnd 1 - Option 1 and Rnd 2 following instructions on pages 7 and 8.

Rnd 3: Ch 1, *sc in next 3 sc, ch 2, sk next 3 sc, [dc, ch 2] 3 times in next sc, sk next 3 sc; repeat from * around. Join with sl st to beg sc.

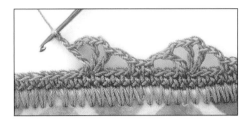

Rnd 4: Ch 1, sk 1st sc, *sc in next sc, sk next sc and ch 2, **4 dc in next ch-2 space between 2 dc, ch 2; repeat from ** in next ch-2 space, sk next ch 2 and next sc, sc in next sc; repeat from * around. Join with sl st to beg ch. You may continue with Rnd 5 or you may fasten off at the end of this round.

Rnd 5: This round is optional. Ch 2, sk next 2 chs, *sc in next 4 dc, 3 sc in ch-2 space, sc in next 4 dc, ch 2, sk next 4 chs; rep from * around. Join with sl st to beg ch. Fasten off. Weave in ends. Block.

XoXo

SHOPPING LIST

Thread (Size 10)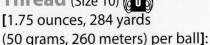
[1.75 ounces, 284 yards
(50 grams, 260 meters) per ball]:
- ☐ Color #1 (Grey) - 1 ball
- ☐ Color #2 (Brown) - 1 ball

Crochet Hooks
- ☐ Edgit™ Piercing Hook **and**
- ☐ Edgit™ Crochet Hook

Additional Supplies
- ☐ See page 4, Basic Tools & Supplies

INSTRUCTIONS

Note: Use the Edgit™ Piercing Crochet Hook to work Foundation Rnd 1; switch to the Edgit™ Crochet Hook for Rnds 2-3.

Foundation Rnds 1 and 2: With color #1, crochet Foundation Rnd 1 - Option 1 and Rnd 2 following instructions on pages 7 and 8. Fasten off. Attach color #2.

STITCH GUIDE

"O"
(Sc, ch 3, sc) in st indicated.

"X"
To make the first "stick" of the "X", work sc in the base of next sc *(see Photo A)*; to make the second "stick" of the "X", work sc in the base of the sc to the right of the first "stick" crossing over it *(see Photo B)*.

Photo A

Rnd 3: This pattern is made of "Os" and "Xs" *(see Stitch Guide)*. Ch 1, *sc in next 2 sc, make the "O" in next sc, sc in next 2 sc; make the "X" using next sc*, repeat from * to * around. Join with sl st to beg sc. Fasten off. Weave in ends. Block.

Photo B

Rockabye

SHOPPING LIST

Thread (Size 10) [LACE 0]
[1.75 ounces, 284 yards
(50 grams, 260 meters) per ball]:
☐ 1 Ball

Crochet Hooks
☐ Edgit™ Piercing Hook **and**
☐ Edgit™ Crochet Hook

Additional Supplies
☐ ½" (12 mm) Wide ribbon:
for burp cloth, 1½ yards
(1.5 meters); for blanket,
5 yards (4.5 meters)
☐ Safety pin
☐ Sewing needle and thread
☐ See page 4, Basic Tools &
Supplies

INSTRUCTIONS

Note: Use the Edgit™ Piercing
Crochet Hook to work
Foundation Rnd 1; switch to the
Edgit™ Crochet Hook for Rnds
2-4.

Foundation Rnds 1 and 2:
Crochet Foundation Rnd 1 -
Option 1 and Rnd 2 following
instructions on pages 7 and 8.

Rnd 3: Ch 2 (counts as 1st dc), *ch 4, dc in same sc, sk 3 sc, dc in next sc*; repeat from * to * around. Join with sl st to beg st.

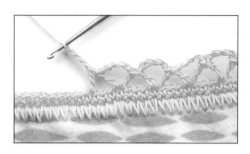

Rnd 4: Ch 1, sc in ch-4 space, work *[7 dc, ch 2, 7 dc] in next ch-4 space, sl st in next ch-4 space; repeat from * around. Join with sl st to beg sc. Fasten off. Weave in ends. Block.

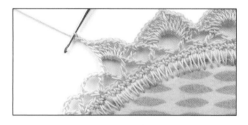

RIBBON INSTRUCTIONS

For burp, cut a piece of ribbon 52" (132 cm) long. Hook a safety pin on one end and weave through each chain space of Rnd 3; sew ends together or tie in a bow. For blanket, cut four strands of ribbon, each 45" (114.5 cm) long. Hook a safety pin to one end of a strand and thread through the ch-3 spaces of Rnd 3, repeat with the other three sides. Tie a bow at each corner where the ends meet.

Tiny Back Steps

Our Tiny Back Steps pattern will test your crochet senses. You will have to go backwards, working from left to right. I'm sure you'll have fond memories of walking backwards as a child. Enjoy!

INSTRUCTIONS

Note: Use the Edgit™ Piercing Crochet Hook to work Foundation Rnd 1, switch to the Edgit™ Crochet Hook for Rnds 2-3 for Thread version, or to B/1-2.25mm for Yarn version.

Foundation Rnds 1 and 2:
Crochet Foundation Rnd 1 - Option 1 and Rnd 2 following instructions on pages 7 and 8.

More Notes: Traditionally you crochet from right to left. In this pattern, you will work from left to right.

Yarn Only - Rnd 3
Ch 1, sc in the first sc to your right, *sk next sc, sc in next sc to your right *, rep from * to * around. Join with sl st to beg sc. Fasten off. Weave in ends. Block.

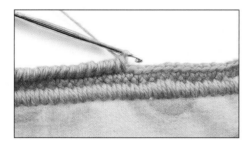

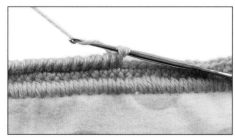

Thread Only - Rnd 3
If you choose to do this pattern with crochet cotton instead of fingering yarn, follow these instructions: Ch 1, sc in the first sc to your right, and in every sc around. Join with sl st to beg sc. Fasten off. Weave in ends. Block.

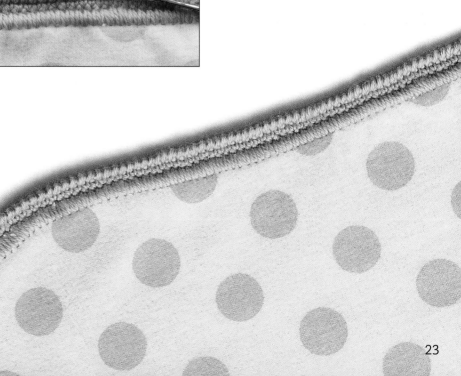

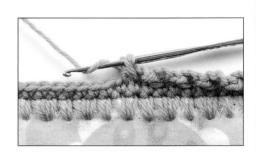

Twist 'n Twirls

INSTRUCTIONS

Note: Use the Edgit™ Piercing
Crochet Hook to work Foundation
Rnd 1- Option 3; switch to the
Edgit™ Crochet Hook for Rnds 2-3.

Foundation Rnds 1 and 2:
Crochet Foundation Rnd 1 -
Option 3 and Rnd 2 following
instructions on page 8.

Rnd 3: *Ch 3, sk next sc, sl st in
next sc, sc in sc to the right of sl st
just made; repeat from * around;
end with sc in sc after beginning
ch-3. Join with sl st to beg ch-1.
Fasten off. Weave in ends. Do not
block.

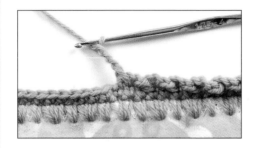

Cony's Tip
To achieve this look, you will need to use the
yarn specified. if you work this stitch with crochet
cotton, it will not have the same look or effect.

Baby Shower Edgings

These one-of-a-kind designs are as pretty as they are practical. Crochet them on fun flannel prints using yarns and crochet cottons in delicious candy colors.

Lil' Sunshine

INSTRUCTIONS

Note: Use the Edgit™ Piercing
Crochet Hook to work Foundation
Rnd 1; switch to the Edgit™
Crochet Hook for Rnd 2.

Foundation Rnd 1: Sc in first hole,
sk next hole, sc in next hole,
repeat from * to * around. Join
with sl st to beg sc.

Rnd 2: Ch 1, sl st in first sc, *ch 1,
sl st in next sc*, repeat from * to *
around. Join with sl st to beg ch.
Fasten off.

Weave in ends. Block.

Pattern Variation (Optional)
You may choose to crochet
Foundation Round 2, page 8, if
desired.

Cony's Tip
Care instructions:
wash in cold water, gentle
cycle, machine dry on cool
setting or hang dry.
For soiled blankets, use
a stain remover spray
or pre-soak them
before washing with
a mild detergent.

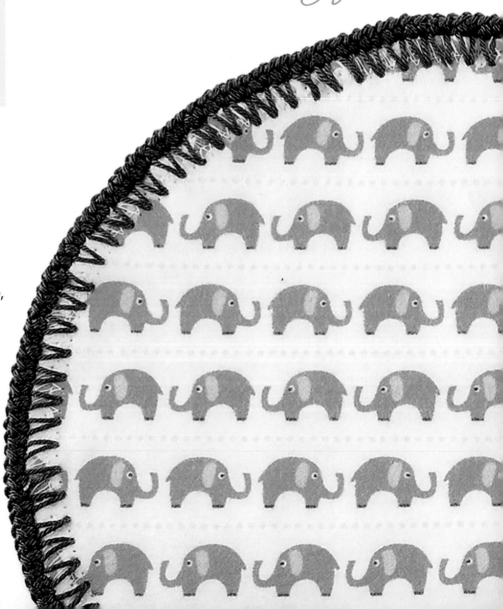

Sophia

Thread (Size 10)
[1.75 ounces, 284 yards
(50 grams, 260 meters) per ball]:
☐ 1 Ball

Crochet Hooks
☐ Edgit™ Piercing Hook **and**
☐ Edgit™ Crochet Hook

Additional Supplies
☐ ¼" (7 mm) Wide ribbon:
   for burp cloth, 1½ yards
   (1.5 meters); for 36" (91.5 cm)
   square blanket, 5 yards
   (4.5 meters)
☐ Small safety pin
☐ Sewing needle and thread
☐ See page 4, Basic Tools &
   Supplies

INSTRUCTIONS
Note: Use the Edgit™ Piercing
Crochet Hook to work Foundation
Rnd 1; switch to the Edgit™
Crochet Hook for Rnds 2-5.

Foundation Rnd 1: Ch 1, sc in
same st, sc in next 8 holes, *2 sc
in next hole, sc in next 9 holes *,
repeat from * to * around. Join
with sl st to beg sc.

Foundation Rnd 2: Ch 1, sc in
each sc around. Join with sl st to
beg sc.

Rnd 3: Turn (back of blanket is
facing you). **Crochet this round
in front loops of Rnd 2.** Ch 1, sc in
same st, *sk next sc, 5 dc in next
sc, sk next sc, sc in next sc*; repeat
from * to * around. Join with sl st
to beg sc.

Rnd 4: Turn (front of blanket is
facing you). **Crochet this round in
back loops of Rnd 2.** Ch 2, dc in
same stitch, dc in each back loop
around. Join with sl st to beg dc.

Rnd 5: Ch 1, sc in same st, sk next
dc, *5 dc in next dc, sk next dc, sc
in next dc, sk next dc*; repeat from
* to * around. Join with a sl st to
beg sc. Fasten off. Weave in ends.

Thread ribbon over and then
under every other 2 dcs from
Rnd 4 (see photo below). Use a
small safety pin at the end of the
ribbon to make it easier to thread
through the dc spaces. Tie a bow
where ends meet. Block.

Ethan

SHOPPING LIST

Thread (Size 10) 🧵 **0** LACE
[1.75 ounces, 284 yards
(50 grams, 260 meters) per ball]:
☐ 1 Ball

Yarn (Light Weight) 🧶 **3** LIGHT
[1.75 ounces, 126 yards
(50 grams, 115 meters) per ball]:
☐ Color #1 (Red) - 1 Ball
☐ Color #2 (Dk Blue) - 1 Ball

Crochet Hooks
☐ Edgit™ Piercing Hook
☐ Edgit™ Crochet Hook **and**
☐ Size B/1 (2.25 mm)

Additional Supplies
☐ See page 4, Basic Tools & Supplies

INSTRUCTIONS

Note: Use the Edgit™ Piercing Crochet Hook to work Foundation Row 1; switch to the Edgit™ Crochet Hook for Rnd 2; work Rnds 3-4 with hook size B/1 (2.25 mm).

Foundation Rnds 1 and 2: Crochet Foundation Rnd 1 - Option 1 and Rnd 2 following instructions on pages 7 and 8, using crochet cotton.

Note: This is a spin-off of Tiny Back Steps on page 23; read that pattern for additional notes. To create this pattern, you will need to keep your tension very loose to make sure your edge won't start to curl. If you can't adjust your tension, try switching to a bigger size crochet hook; go up one or two sizes, whatever works best for you.

Rnd 3: Crochet towards your right. Ch 1, sc in first sc to your right; *ch 1, sk next sc, sc in next sc*; repeat from * to * around. Join with sl st to beg sc. Fasten off color #1.

Rnd 4: Attach yarn color #2. Crochet towards your right. Ch 2, *sk next sc, sc in next skipped sc from Rnd 3, ch 1*; repeat from * to * around. Join with sl st to beg ch. Fasten off. Weave in ends. Block.

Noah

SHOPPING LIST

Thread (Size 10) **LACE 0**
**[1.75 ounces, 284 yards
(50 grams, 260 meters) per ball]:**
☐ Color #1 (Yellow) - 1 Ball
☐ Color #2 (Blue) - 1 Ball

Crochet Hooks
☐ Edgit™ Piercing Hook **and**
☐ Edgit™ Crochet Hook

Additional Supplies
☐ See page 4, Basic Tools &
Supplies

INSTRUCTIONS

Note: Use the Edgit™ Piercing
Crochet Hook to work Foundation
Row 1; switch to the Edgit™
Crochet Hook for Rnds 2-4.

Foundation Rnd 1: With color #1,
crochet Foundation Rnd 1 - Option
1 following instructions on page 7.

Rnd 2: Ch 1, sc in same st, *ch 1, sk next sc, sc in next sc*; repeat from * to * around. Join with sl st to beg sc. Do not fasten off.

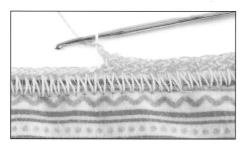

Rnd 3: Attach color #2 in 1st ch-1 space; ch 1, 2 sc in same ch-1 space, *ch 1, sk next sc, 2 sc in next ch-1 space; repeat from * around, end with ch 1. Join with sl st to beg sc. Fasten off color #2.

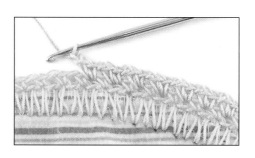

Rnd 4: Pick up color #1. Ch 2, sk 1st 2 sc, *2 sc in ch-1 space, ch 1, sk next 2 sc; repeat from * around. Join with sl st to beg sc. Fasten off. Weave in ends. Block.

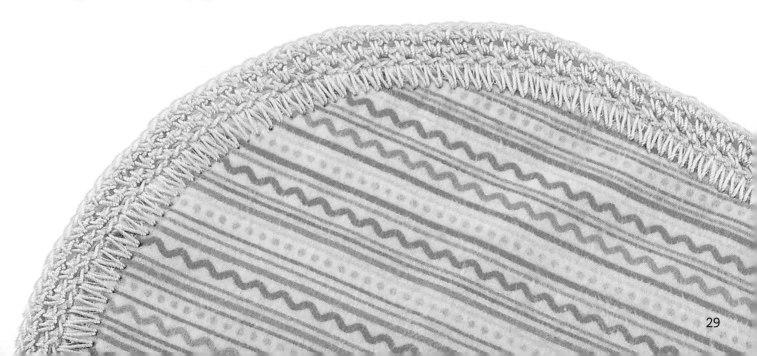

Olivia

INSTRUCTIONS

Note: Use the Edgit™ Piercing
Crochet Hook to work Foundation
Row 1; switch to the Edgit™
Crochet Hook for Rnds 2-4.

Foundation Rnds 1 and 2:
Crochet Foundation Rnd 1 -
Option 1 and Rnd 2 following
instructions on pages 7 and 8,
using crochet cotton.

Rnd 3: Attach yarn color #1. Ch 1,
sc in same st and in the next 2 sc,
ch 1, sk next sc, sc in next 3 sc;
repeat from * to * around. Join
with sl st to beg sc. Fasten off
color #1.

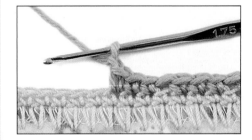

Rnd 4: Attach yarn color #2 to a
ch-1 space, sc in same ch-1 space,
ch 4, *sk next 3 sc, sc in ch-1 space,
ch 4; repeat from * around. Join
with sl st to beg sc. Fasten off.
Weave in ends. Block.

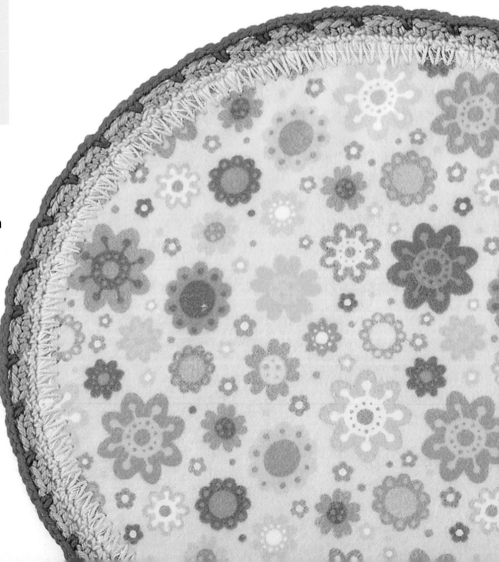

Aiden

31

SHOPPING LIST

Thread (Size 10) **0** LACE
[1.75 ounces, 284 yards
(50 grams, 260 meters) per ball]:
☐ MC (Green) - 1 Ball
☐ CC (Brown) - 1 Ball

Crochet Hooks
☐ Edgit™ Piercing Hook **and**
☐ Edgit™ Crochet Hook

Additional Supplies
☐ See page 4, Basic Tools &
Supplies

INSTRUCTIONS

Note: Use the Edgit™ Piercing
Crochet Hook to work Foundation
Row 1; switch to the Edgit™
Crochet Hook for Rnds 2-3.

Foundation Rnd 1: With main
color, crochet Foundation Rnd 1 -
Option 2, page 8, around. Fasten
off. Attach contrasting color.

Rnd 2: Ch 1, sc in same st, sc in
next sc, *ch 1, sk next sc, sc in next
2 sc, sc in hole **below** from Rnd 1,
sc in next 2 sc*; repeat from * to *
around. Join with sl st to beg sc.
Fasten off. Attach main color to 1st
sc of Rnd 2.

Rnd 3: Ch 1, sc in same st, sc
in next sc, * sc in sc from Rnd 1
(**below** ch-1 space), sc in next 5
sc*; repeat from * to * around.
Join with sl st to beg sc. Fasten off.
Weave in ends. Block.

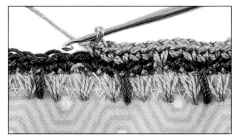

On the Edge Crochet

These tiny patterns make sweet edgings for a variety of projects. Every stitch is designed to express love for the babies and children in our lives.

Very Berry

Yarn (Super Fine Weight) **1** SUPER FINE
[3.5 ounces, 437 yards
(100 grams, 400 meters) per
skein]:

☐ 1 Skein
You may also use any yarn
that will yield 7-8 sts per inch
(2.5 cm).

Crochet Hooks
☐ Edgit™ Piercing Hook **and**
☐ Edgit™ Crochet Hook

Additional Supplies
☐ See page 4, Basic Tools &
Supplies

INSTRUCTIONS

Note: Use the Edgit™ Piercing
Crochet Hook to work Foundation
Rnd 1, switch to the Edgit™
Crochet Hook for Rnd 2.

Foundation Rnd 1: Crochet
Foundation Rnd 1 - Option 2
following instructions on page 8.

STITCH GUIDE

BERRY
Insert hook in st indicated, *yo
and pull up a loop, [yo and draw
through 1 loop on hook]* 3
more times *(see Photo A*, making
sure to keep the ch-3 just
made in front of your work), yo
and draw through both loops
on hook *(see Photo B)*, berry
completed!

Photo A

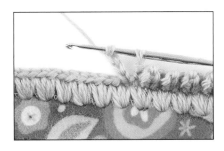

Photo B

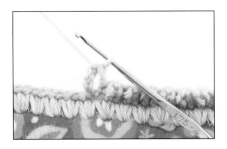

Rnd 2: Ch 1, sc in first sc, *crochet
a berry *(see Stitch Guide)* in next
sc, sc in next sc, repeat from *
around. Join with sl st to beg sc.
Fasten off. Weave in ends. Block.

Dainty Blossoms

Yarn (Super Fine Weight) [3.5 ounces, 437 yards (100 grams, 400 meters) per skein]:

☐ Color #1 (Pink) - 1 Skein
☐ Color #2 (Green) - 1 Skein
You may also use any yarn that will yield 7-8 sts per inch (2.5 cm).

Crochet Hooks

☐ Edgit™ Piercing Hook **and**
☐ Edgit™ Crochet Hook

Additional Supplies

☐ See page 4, Basic Tools & Supplies

INSTRUCTIONS

Note: Use the Edgit™ Piercing Crochet Hook to work Foundation Rnd 1; switch to the Edgit™ Crochet Hook for Rnds 2-4.

Foundation Rnds 1 and 2: With color #1, crochet Foundation Rnd 1 - Option 1 and Rnd 2 following instructions on pages 7 and 8.

STITCH GUIDE

SPIKE SC *(abbreviated Ssc)*

Insert hook in corresponding st 1 rnd **below** next st, yo, pull up loop to height of current rnd, yo, pull through 2 loops on hook.

LEAF CLUSTER

Work (Ssc, ch 6) 2 times in indicated st, work Ssc in same st.

BLOSSOM

Work 5 dc in indicated st, insert your hook through the back of 1st dc *(see Photo B)* and close with sl st, blossom completed.

Repeat Pattern

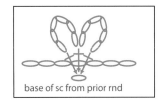

base of sc from prior rnd

Key Guide

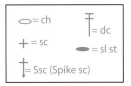

◠ = ch ⊤ = dc
+ = sc ➤ = sl st
⊤ = Ssc (Spike sc)

Rnd 3: With color #2, ch 1, *sc in next 3 sc, work Ssc *(see Stitch Guide)*, sc in next 3 sc, make a leaf cluster in next sc* *(see Stitch Guide)*, repeat from * to * around. Join with sl st to beg sc. Fasten off.

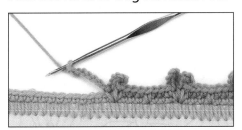

Rnd 4: With color #1, ch 1, sl st in back loop only of first 7 sc, *sk 1st Ssc of leaf cluster, crochet a blossom in center Ssc *(see Photos A & B)*, sk next Ssc, sl st in back loop only of next 7 sc*, repeat from * to * around. Join with sl st to beg st. Fasten off. Weave in ends. Block.

Photo A

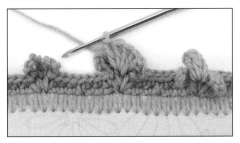

Photo B

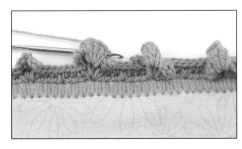

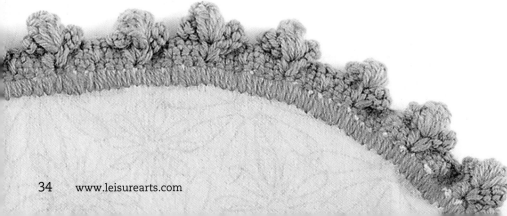

Sweet Lullaby

Sweet Lullaby is an excellent pattern for beginners.
Crochet on a soft, high-quality flannel for a good night's rest for baby.

SHOPPING LIST

Yarn (Super Fine Weight) **SUPER FINE 1**
**[3.5 ounces, 437 yards
(100 grams, 400 meters) per
skein]:**

☐ 1 Skein
You may also use any yarn
that will yield 7-8 sts per inch
(2.5 cm).

Crochet Hooks
☐ Edgit™ Piercing Hook **and**
☐ Size B/1 (2.25 mm)

Additional Supplies
☐ See page 4, Basic Tools &
Supplies

INSTRUCTIONS

Note: Use the Edgit™ Piercing
Crochet Hook to work Foundation
Rnd 1; switch to hook size B/1
(2.25 mm) for Rnd 2.

Foundation Rnd 1: Crochet
Foundation Rnd 1 - Option 2
following instructions on page 8.

Rnd 2: Ch 1, sl st in first sc, *dc in
next sc, sl st in next sc*, repeat
from * to * around. Join with sl
st to beg ch. Fasten off. Weave in
ends. Block.

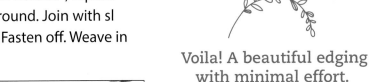

Voila! A beautiful edging
with minimal effort.

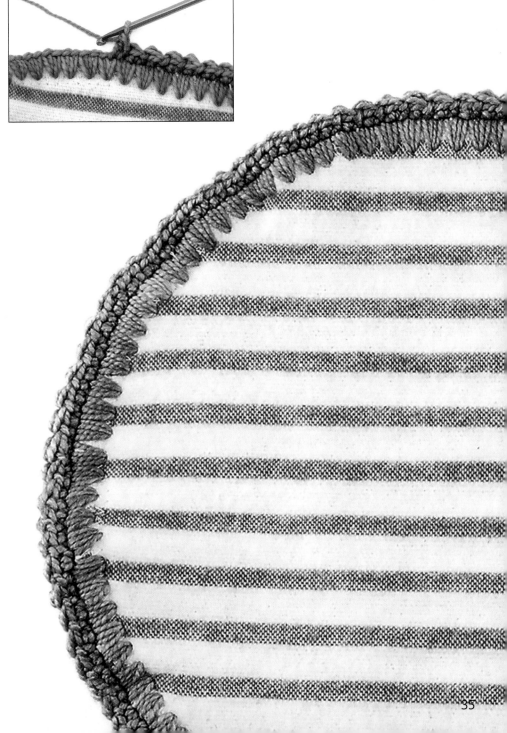

All Bliss

 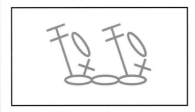
STITCH GUIDE
BLISS CLUSTER

(Sc, ch 1, dc) in st indicated.

Bliss Cluster Repeat Pattern

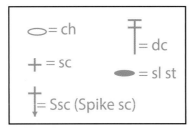

Key Guide

○ = ch
+ = sc
⊤ = Ssc (Spike sc)
T = dc
● = sl st

Rnd 2: Ch 1, crochet a Bliss cluster
(see Stitch Guide) in first sc, *sk
next sc, Bliss cluster in next sc*,
repeat from * to * around. Join
with sl st to beg sc. Fasten off.

Weave in ends. Block.

Pattern Variation (Optional)
You may choose to crochet
Foundation Round 2, page 8, if
desired.

INSTRUCTIONS

Note: Use the Edgit™ Piercing
Crochet Hook to work Foundation
Rnd 1; switch to hook size B/1
(2.25 mm) for Rnd 2.

Foundation Rnd 1: Crochet
Foundation Rnd 1 - Option 2
following instructions on page 8.

Soft Cuddles

SHOPPING LIST

Thread (Size 10)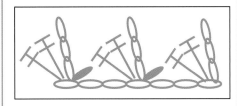
**[1.75 ounces, 284 yards
(50 grams, 260 meters) per ball]:**
☐ 1 Ball

Crochet Hooks
☐ Edgit™ Piercing Hook **and**
☐ Edgit™ Crochet Hook

Additional Supplies
☐ See page 4, Basic Tools &
   Supplies

INSTRUCTIONS
Note: Use the Edgit™ Piercing
Crochet Hook to work Foundation
Rnd 1; switch to the Edgit™
Crochet Hook for Rnds 2-3.

Foundation Rnds 1 and 2:
Crochet Foundation Rnd 1 -
Option 1 and Rnd 2 following
instructions on pages 7 and 8.

STITCH GUIDE
CUDDLE CLUSTER
(Sl st, ch 3, 2 dc) in indicated st.

Cuddle Cluster Repeat Pattern

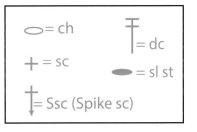

Key Guide

◯ = ch

+ = sc

↧ = Ssc (Spike sc)

⊤ = dc

⬮ = sl st

Rnd 3: Ch 3 (**counts as 1ˢᵗ dc**), 2 dc
in first sc, *sk 2 sc, work Cuddle
Cluster *(see Stitch Guide)* in next
sc*, repeat from * to * around. Join
with sl st to beg ch 3. Fasten off.
Weave in ends. Block.

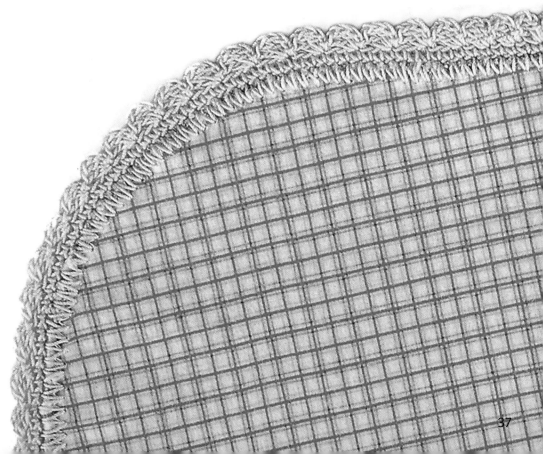

Just Dreamy

 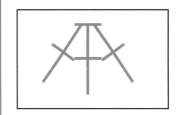
INSTRUCTIONS

Note: Use the Edgit™ Piercing
Crochet Hook to work Foundation
Rnd 1; switch to the Edgit™
Crochet Hook for Rnds 2-4.

Foundation Rnds 1 and 2:
Crochet Foundation Rnd 1 -
Option 1 and Rnd 2 following
instructions on pages 7 and 8.

STITCH GUIDE
DC3TOG CLUSTER
*Yo, insert hook in st indicated,
yo and draw up a loop, yo, draw
through 2 loops on hook*,
repeat from * to * 2 **more** times in
the same stitch; you should have
4 loops left on your hook *(see
photo A)*, yo and draw thread
through all loops, ch 3, repeat
from * to * one more time in the
same stitch; cluster completed.

Dc3tog Cluster Repeat Pattern

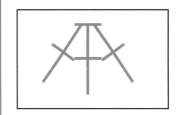

Rnd 3: Ch 2, make a cluster in first
sc *(see Stitch Guide)*, *sk next 3 sc,
work a cluster in next sc*, repeat
from * to * around. Join with sl st
to beg dc.

Photo A

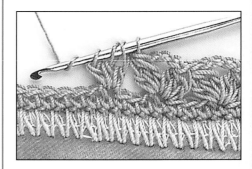

Rnd 4: Ch 1, sk first dc3tog, 5 sc in
ch-3 space of cluster from Rnd 3,
*sl st between clusters, 5 sc in next
ch-3 sp*, repeat from * to * around.
Join with sl st to beg ch. Fasten off.
Weave in ends. Block.

Just Dreamy Edgings

These colorful patterns are perfect for embellishing a wide range of projects. Let these projects be your source of inspiration, and indulge your creative appetite while you crochet gifts for those you love.

African Flower

SHOPPING LIST

Thread (Size 10)
[1.75 ounces, 284 yards (50 grams, 260 meters) per ball]:
- ☐ Color A - 1 Ball
- ☐ Color B -20 yards (18.5 meters)

Crochet Hooks
- ☐ Edgit™ Piercing Hook **and**
- ☐ Edgit™ Crochet Hook

Additional Supplies
- ☐ See page 4, Basic Tools & Supplies

INSTRUCTIONS

Note: Use the Edgit™ Piercing Crochet Hook to work Foundation Rnd 1; switch to the Edgit™ Crochet Hook for Rnds 2-4.

Foundation Rnds 1 and 2: Crochet Foundation Rnd 1 - Option 1 and Rnd 2 following instructions on pages 7 and 8.

STITCH GUIDE

SPIKE SC
Insert hook in corresponding st 1 row below next st, yo, pull up loop to height of current row, yo, pull through 2 loops on hook.

Rnd 3: Ch 3 (counts as first dc), 5 dc in 1st sc, *sk next 4 sc, 6 dc in next sc; repeat from * around. Join with sl st to beg ch 3. Fasten off. Weave in ends.

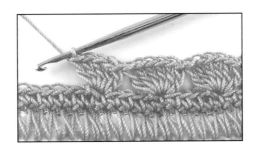

Rnd 4: Join color B to 1st dc, ch 1, sc in 1st dc, sc in next 5 dcs, *Spike Sc in 2nd sc below in Rnd 2 (between sets of 6 dcs), sc in next 6 dcs; repeat from * around, end with Spike Sc after last 6 dcs. Join with sl st to beg sc. Fasten off. Weave in ends. Block.

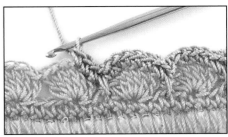

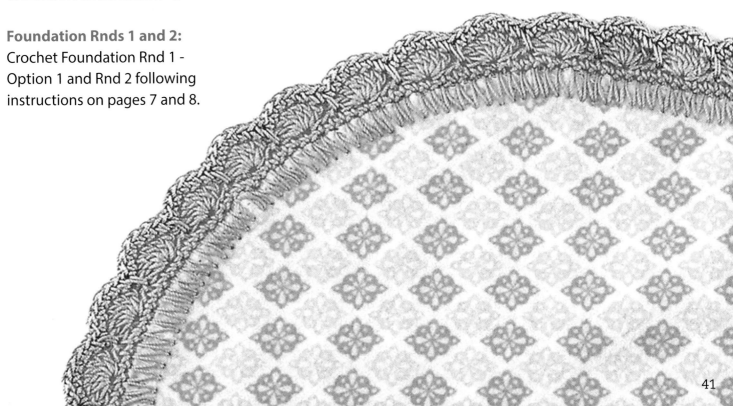

Crescent Seashells Apron

SHOPPING LIST

Thread (Size 8)
[.35 ounces, 87 yards
(10 grams, 79.5 meters) per ball]:
- ☐ 2 Balls

Crochet Hooks
- ☐ Edgit™ Piercing Hook **and**
- ☐ Edgit™ Crochet Hook

Additional Supplies
- ☐ See page 4, Basic Tools & Supplies.

STITCH GUIDE
CRESCENT SHELL
(abbreviated CS)

(3 Sc, 2 hdc, 3 dc, 3 tr) in ch-5 space indicated.

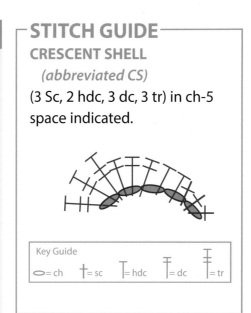

Key Guide

◯ = ch   ┬ = sc   ┳ = hdc   ┰ = dc   ┲ = tr

Row 3: *Ch 5, sk 4 scs, sl st in next sc, ch 3, sk 2 scs, sl st in next sc; repeat from * across, end with ch 3, sk 2 scs, sl st in last sc. Fasten off.

Row 4: Join crochet cotton to beg sc from Row 3. Work CS *(see Stitch Guide)* in first ch-5 space, *sk next ch-3 space, sl st in next sl st, CS in next ch-5 space; repeat from * across. Join with sl st to beg sc. Fasten off. Weave in ends. Block.

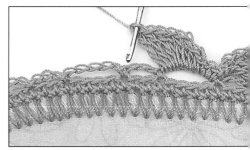

Crochet Cotton #8 is very thin; we put two strands together to work this pattern. You may use DMC #10 if desired.

INSTRUCTIONS

Note: Use the Edgit™ Piercing Crochet Hook to work Foundation Row 1; switch to the Edgit™ Crochet Hook for Rows 2-4.

Foundation Row 1: Starting on the bottom right corner of apron, join crochet cotton to first st, work Foundation Rnd 1- Option 2, page 8, across. Fasten off.

Foundation Row 2: With **right** side facing you, join crochet cotton to beg sc from Row 1; sc in each sc across, ch 1, turn.

Reversible Bandana Pocket Full of Posies

SHOPPING LIST

Thread (Size 10) 0 LACE
[1.75 ounces, 284 yards (50 grams, 260 meters) per ball]:
☐ 1 Ball

Crochet Hooks
☐ Edgit™ Piercing Hook **and**
☐ Edgit™ Crochet Hook

Additional Supplies
☐ See page 4, Basic Tools & Supplies

This is a double-sided bandana; the edging is reversible so you can use the bandana on both sides; start with Side A facing you.

INSTRUCTIONS

Note: Use the Edgit™ Piercing Crochet Hook to work Foundation Row 1; switch to the Edgit™ Crochet Hook for Rows 2-3.

Foundation Row 1: Using your zigzag stitches as a guide and starting on the right corner of bandana on Side A, join crochet cotton to first st, ch 1, sc in same st, *ch 1, sk next st, sc in next st; repeat from * across, ch 1, turn.

STITCH GUIDE
POSY (abbreviated PS)
(3 Dc, ch 2, sl st, ch 2) 5 times in stitch indicated, end with sl st in back of PS in the same indicated st.

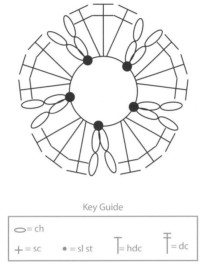

Key Guide

⬮ = ch	
+ = sc	• = sl st	⊤ = hdc	⟙ = dc

Foundation Row 2: Side B of bandana should be facing you; sc in same zigzag st as last sc from Row 1, *ch 1, sk next st, sc in next st; repeat from * across, ch 1, turn. See picture below.

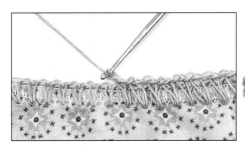

Row 3: Sc in first 2 sts, if you are making the bandana, otherwise, proceed with *ch 8, work a PS *(see Stitch Guide)* in 3rd ch from hook, ch 3, sk 5 sts, sl st in next st, [ch 5, sl st in 3rd ch from hook to form a Picot, ch 2, sk 3 sts, sl st in next st] twice; repeat from * across. If necessary, adjust the number of stitches when you go around corners and towards the end of the row to end row with a PS and sc in last 2 sts. Fasten off. Weave in ends. Block.

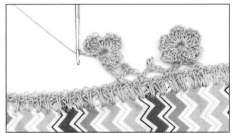

Butterfly Wings Pillowcase

STITCH GUIDE
BUTTERFLY WINGS
(abbreviated BW)
(3 Dc, ch 2, sl st, ch 2, 3 dc) in
stitch indicated.

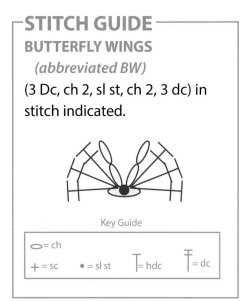

Key Guide

⬮ = ch			
+ = sc	• = sl st	┬ = hdc	┬ = dc

Crochet Cotton #8 is very thin;
make sure to tighten your tension
to avoid stitches looking "loopy".

Rnd 3: Ch 1, *sk 3 sts, work a BW
(see Stitch Guide) in next st, sk
next 3 sts, sl st in next st, ch 2, sk
next st, sl st in next st; repeat from
* around. Join with sl st to beg ch.
Fasten off. Weave in ends. Block.

INSTRUCTIONS
Note: Use the Edgit™ Piercing
Crochet Hook to work Foundation
Rnd 1; switch to the Edgit™
Crochet Hook for Rnds 2-3.

Foundation Rnd 1: With right
side facing you, using your zigzag
stitches as a guide, and starting
at the seam of pillowcase, join
crochet cotton to first st, ch 1, 3 sc
in same st, *sk next st, 3 sc in next
st; repeat from * around. Join with
sl st to beg sc.

Foundation Rnd 2: Ch 1, sc in first
sc, *ch 1, sk next st, sc in next st;
repeat from * around. Join with sl
st to beg sc.

Rosebloom Cross Fans

SHOPPING LIST

Yarn (Super Fine Weight) **SUPER FINE 1**
**[3.5 ounces, 437 yards
(100 grams, 400 meters) per
skein]:**

☐ 1 Skein
You may also use any yarn
that will yield 7-8 sts per inch
(2.5 cm).

Crochet Hooks

☐ Edgit™ Piercing Hook **and**
☐ Edgit™ Crochet Hook

Additional Supplies

☐ See page 4, Basic Tools &
Supplies

INSTRUCTIONS

Note: Use the Edgit™ Piercing
Crochet Hook to work Foundation
Rnd 1; switch to the Edgit™
Crochet Hook for Rnds 2-3 or use
hook size B/1 (2.25 mm) if desired.

Foundation Rnds 1 and 2: With
right side facing you, using your
zigzag stitches as a guide, and
starting on any side of the quilt,
join crochet cotton to first st, work
Foundation Rnd 1 - Option 2 and
Rnd 2, page 8, around. Join with
sl st to beg sc.

Rnd 3: Ch 1, sc in first sc, *ch 2, 4
dc in sc to the right of sc just made
(you will be crossing over the prior
sc), sk 4 sts, sc in next st; repeat from
* around. Join with sl st to beg sc.
Fasten off. Weave in ends. Block.

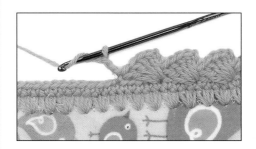

Cony's VERY IMPORTANT TIP!
All patterns can be worked in rows or rounds. If
you are working the pattern in rounds, such as
for blankets, bibs, burps, pillowcases, dresses,
skirts, etc., remember to join with sl st to beg st
at the end of every round.

Apple Green
Trellis Summer Dress

INSTRUCTIONS

Note: Use the Edgit™ Piercing
Crochet Hook to work Foundation
Rnd 1; switch to the Edgit™
Crochet Hook for Rnds 2-5 or use
hook size B/1 (2.25 mm) if desired.

Foundation Rnd 1: With **right**
side facing you, using your zigzag
stitches as a guide, and starting on
any side of bottom hem of dress,
join yarn to first st, ch 1, sc in same
st, sc in each st around. Join with sl
st to beg sc.

Rnd 2: *Ch 2, sk next sc, sl st in
next sc; repeat from * around. Join
with sl st to beg ch.

Rnd 3: *Ch 3, sl st in next ch-2
space; repeat from * around. Join
with sl st to beg ch.

Rnd 4: *Ch 4, sl st in next ch-3
space; repeat from * around. Join
with sl st to beg ch.

Rnd 5: *Ch 5, sl st in next ch-4
space; repeat from * around. Join
with sl st to beg ch.

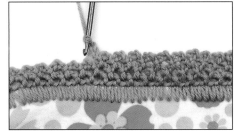

Note: You may continue to add more
rounds by repeating Rnd 5 until you
achieve desired length. You will be
increasing one more ch to the repeat
pattern with each round. Fasten off.
Weave in ends. Block.

Reversible Tulips Peter Pan Collar

SHOPPING LIST

Thread (Size 10) LACE 0
[1.75 ounces, 284 yards (50 grams, 260 meters) per ball]:
☐ 1 Ball

Crochet Hooks
☐ Edgit™ Piercing Hook **and**
☐ Edgit™ Crochet Hook

Additional Supplies
☐ See page 4, Basic Tools & Supplies

INSTRUCTIONS

Note: Use the Edgit™ Piercing Crochet Hook to work Foundation Row 1; switch to the Edgit™ Crochet Hook for Rows 2-5.

Foundation Row 1: With Side A facing, using your zigzag stitches as a guide, and starting on back corner of right section, join crochet cotton to first st, ch 1, sc in same st, sc in each st across to the corner of right section, pick up left section and join right and left sections by working a sc in the first st of left section, sc in each st across to next corner, work 2 sc in last st, ch 1, turn collar so Side B is facing you.

STITCH GUIDE

FAN STITCH *(abbreviated FS)*
(4 Dc, ch 1, 4 dc) in indicated stitch

Foundation Row 2: Sc in same zigzag st as last sc from Row 1, sc in each st across both sections of collar, turn.

Row 3: Ch 5 for the buttonhole if you are making a collar, otherwise proceed to sl st in first sc, sl st in each sc across, ch 1, turn collar so Side B is facing you.

Note: This is a double-sided collar made of two sections, a right section and a left section; the edging is reversible so you can use the collar on both sides; start with Side A facing you. If you are making a blanket, make sure that you work in Rounds rather than Rows, and join with sl st to beg st at the end of each round.

Row 4: Work in front loop only of each sl st; sk 2 sts, *FS *(see Stitch Guide)* in next st, sk 2 sts, sl st in next st, sk 2 sts; repeat from * across to back corner, ch 1, turn collar so Side A is facing you.

Row 5: Working in front loop only of each st, repeat Row 4 across to buttonhole, work 10 sc in ch-5 space. Join with sl st to first st. Fasten off. Weave in ends. Block.

Stitch Guide

Holding the hook

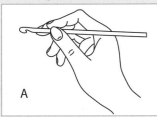

A   B

Holding the yarn

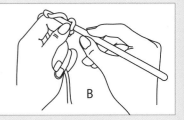

A   B

Slip knot

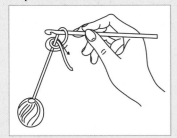

Start with a slip knot on your hook.

Yarn over (yo)

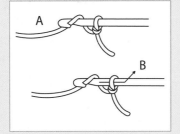

A

B

Yarn over (yo), pull through loop (lp) on hook.

Chain (ch)

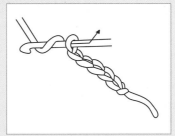

Yarn over (yo), pull through loop (lp) on hook.

Slip stitch (sl st)

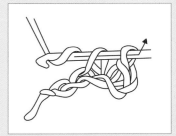

Insert hook in stitch (st), pull through both lps on hook.

Single crochet (sc)

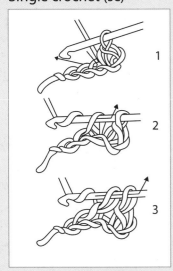

1

2

3

Insert hook in st, yo, pull through st, yo, pull through both lps on hook.

Half double crochet (hdc)

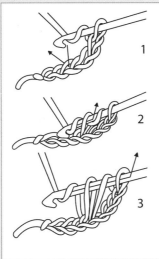

1

2

3

Yo, insert hook in st, yo, pull through st, yo, pull through all 3 lps on hook.

Double crochet (dc)

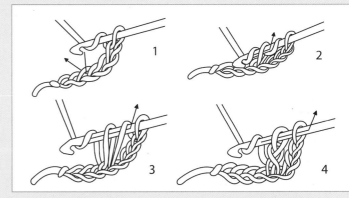

1

2

3

4

Yo, insert hook in st, yo, pull through st, [yo, pull through 2 lps] twice.

Treble crochet (tr)

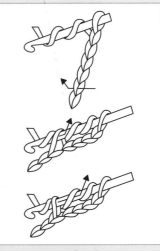

Yo twice, insert hook in st, yo, pull through st, [yo, pull through 2 lps] 3 times.

Double treble crochet (dtr)

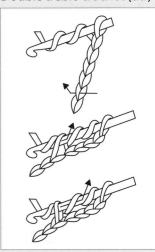

Yo 3 times, insert hook in st, yo, pull through st, [yo, pull through 2 lps] 4 times.

Front/back loop (front lp/back lp)

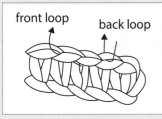

front loop

back loop

Changing colors

To change colors, drop the first color. With the second color, pull through last lp of st.